CONSTELLATIONS
COLORING BOOK

Mrs Mauve

ANDROMEDA

SIZE IN THE NIGHT SKY

BIG

1400 **X** the size of the full moon
times

DID YOU KNOW?

In the Greek legend, Princess Andromeda married the hero Perseus after he saved her from a giant monster whale called Cetus.

BONUS FACT

Cetus is also a constellation, you'll come across it later on the book!

ALPHERATZ

MIRACH

ALMACH

ORIGIN

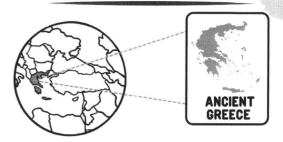

ANCIENT GREECE

BEST TIME TO FIND IT

J	F	M	A
M	J	J	A
S	O	**N**	D

PEGASUS

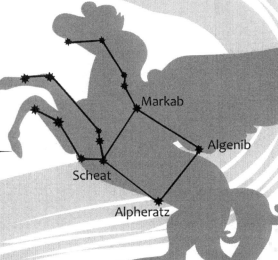

Markab

Algenib

Scheat

Alpheratz

SIZE IN THE NIGHT SKY

HUGE

2174 **X**
times   the size of
the full moon

ORIGIN

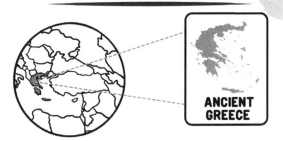

ANCIENT GREECE

DID YOU KNOW?

The legend says that after helping the hero Bellerophon defeat the Chimera, Zeus transformed Pegasus into a constellation as a reward.

BEST TIME TO FIND IT

J F M A
M J J A
S O N D

PERSEUS

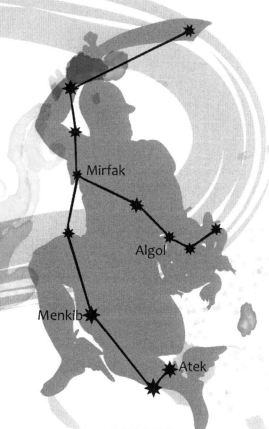

Mirfak

Algol

Menkib

Atek

SIZE IN THE NIGHT SKY

BIG

1192 times **X** the size of the full moon

DID YOU KNOW?

Perseus was a hero who defeated the evil monster Medusa by request of a king.

Medusa was a gorgon, a monster that transformed people into stone by looking at them.

ORIGIN

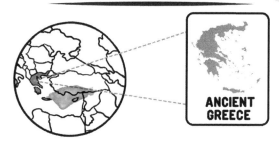

ANCIENT GREECE

BEST TIME TO FIND IT

J	F	M	A
M	J	J	A
S	O	N	**D**

CYGNUS
(swan)

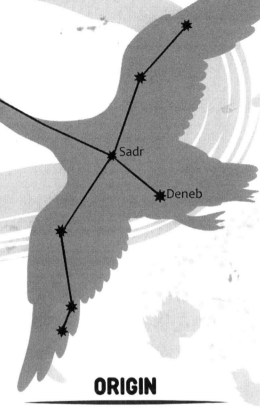

Sadr

Deneb

SIZE IN THE NIGHT SKY

BIG

1559 times **X** the size of the full moon

DID YOU KNOW?

There are so many legendary swans in Greek mythology, that it's impossible to know which one inspired this constellation.

ORIGIN

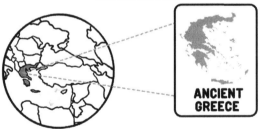

ANCIENT GREECE

BEST TIME TO FIND IT

J	F	M	A
M	J	**J**	**A**
S	**O**	N	D

LIBRA
(the scales)

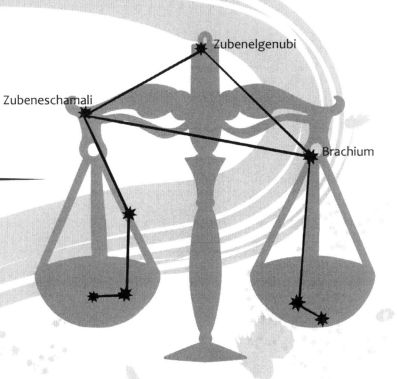

Zubenelgenubi

Zubeneschamali

Brachium

SIZE IN THE NIGHT SKY

BIG

1043 **X**
times   the size of
the full moon

DID YOU KNOW?

The scales were a sacred object of Shamash, the Babylonian god of justice, morality and honesty.

ORIGIN

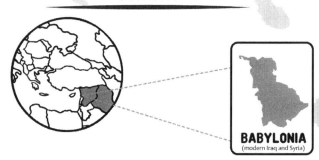

BABYLONIA
(modern Iraq and Syria)

BEST TIME TO FIND IT

J	F	M	A
M	J	J	A
S	O	N	D

CEPHEUS

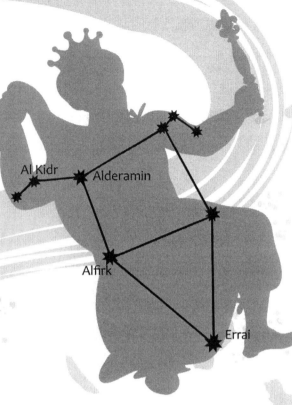

Al Kidr
Alderamin
Alfirk
Errai

SIZE IN THE NIGHT SKY

BIG

1140 **X**
times   the size of the full moon

DID YOU KNOW?

King Cepheus was the father of Princess Andromeda and King of Jaffa.

He and Queen Cassiopeia got into trouble with the god of the sea, Poseidon.

ORIGIN

ANCIENT GREECE

BEST TIME TO FIND IT

J	F	M	A
M	J	J	A
S	O	**N**	D

CRATER
(the cup)

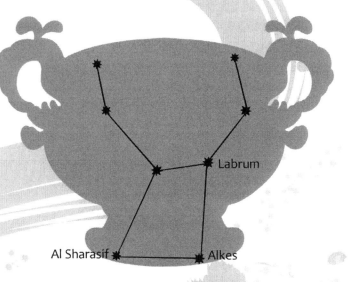

Labrum

Al Sharasif

Alkes

SIZE IN THE NIGHT SKY

TINY

547 times **X** the size of the full moon

DID YOU KNOW?

It was the Babylonians who first combined Crater and Corvus (the crow) into a single constellation. Later the Greeks created the myth of the crow and Apollo.

The legend says Apollo sent the bird to fetch a cup of water. The crow got distracted, then tried to trick Apollo by blaming a snake (Hydra) for its tardiness.

ORIGIN

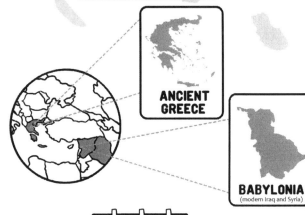

ANCIENT GREECE

BABYLONIA
(modern Iraq and Syria)

BEST TIME TO FIND IT

J F M **A**
M J J A
S O N D

CASSIOPEIA

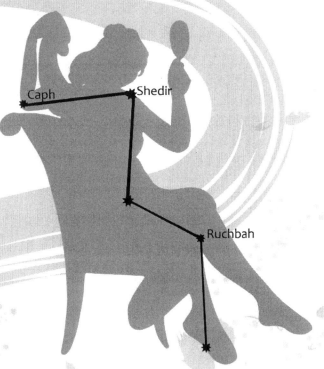

Caph • —Shedir

Ruchbah

SIZE IN THE NIGHT SKY

BIG

1159 **X**
times   the size of
          the full moon

DID YOU KNOW?

Cassiopeia is the mother of Princess Andromeda. After bragging that her daughter was more beautiful than the sea nymphs, Poseidon had Andromeda tied to a rock to be eaten by the monster whale Cetus. She was saved by Perseus before that could happen.

ORIGIN

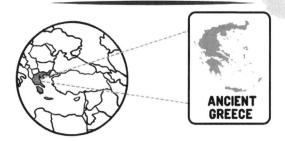

ANCIENT GREECE

BEST TIME TO FIND IT

J	F	M	A
M	J	J	A
S	O	**N**	D

CETUS

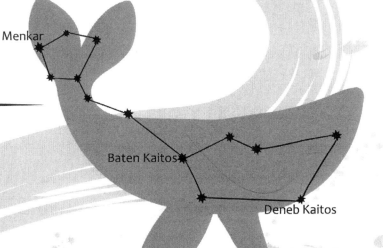

Menkar

Baten Kaitos

Deneb Kaitos

SIZE IN THE NIGHT SKY

HUGE

2387 X
times the size of
the full moon

DID YOU KNOW?

The Mesopotamians associated Cetus with a whale. For the Greeks it represented the sea monster that Perseus saved Princess Andromeda from.

It's easy to see how a whale might look like a monster to ancient people!

ORIGIN

ANCIENT GREECE

MESOPOTAMIA
(Modern Iraq)

BEST TIME TO FIND IT

J	F	M	A
M	J	J	A
S	O	**N**	D

HERCULES

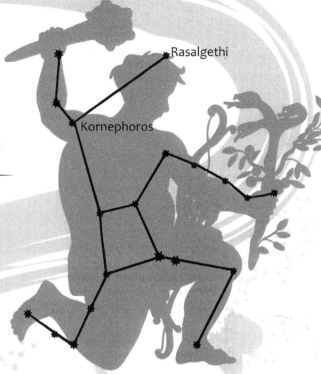

Rasalgethi

Kornephoros

SIZE IN THE NIGHT SKY

HUGE

2375 **X**
times   the size of
the full moon

ORIGIN

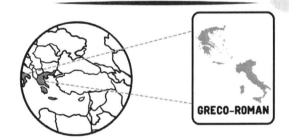

GRECO-ROMAN

DID YOU KNOW?

Hercules (Heracles) is the most famous hero of Greco-Roman mythology . He is known for having done many things, but his most famous adventure is the 12 labors he did for King Eurystheus as penance for a crime.

BEST TIME TO FIND IT

J	F	M	A
M	J	**J**	A
S	O	N	D

LYRA
(lyre)

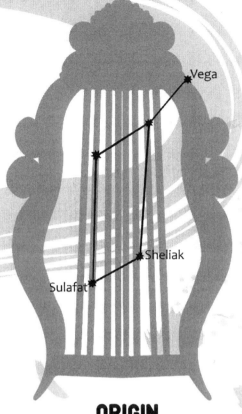

SIZE IN THE NIGHT SKY

TINY

554 times **X** the size of the full moon

DID YOU KNOW?

Lyra represents the first lyre (a musical instrument) ever made. A gift to Apollo from Hermes, who made the lyre using a tortoise shell.

! BONUS FACT

Vega is the fifth brightest star in the sky.

ORIGIN

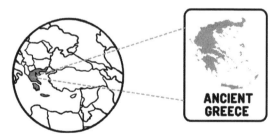

ANCIENT GREECE

BEST TIME TO FIND IT

J	F	M	A
M	J	J	**A**
S	O	N	D

OPHIUCHUS

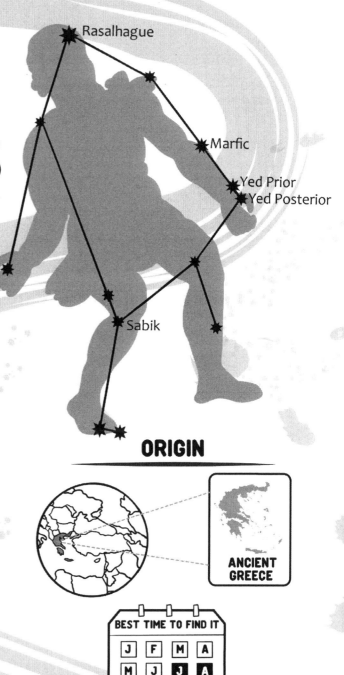

Rasalhague

Marfic

Yed Prior
Yed Posterior

Sabik

SIZE IN THE NIGHT SKY

BIG

1838 times **X** the size of the full moon

DID YOU KNOW?

Ophichus and Serpens are two different constellations that combine to form the single image of a man holding a large snake.

BONUS FACT

To the ancient Greeks, the constellation represented the god Apollo struggling with a huge snake that guarded the Oracle of Delphi.

ORIGIN

ANCIENT GREECE

BEST TIME TO FIND IT

J	F	M	A
M	J	J	A
S	O	N	D

SERPENS

(snake)

Serpens Caput

Unukalhai

Alya

Tang

Serpens Cauda

SIZE IN THE NIGHT SKY

BIG

1235 times **X** the size of the full moon

DID YOU KNOW?

Serpens represents a snake held by the healer Asclepius. Because snakes shed their skin every year, they were known as the symbol of rebirth in ancient Greek society.

ORIGIN

ANCIENT GREECE

BEST TIME TO FIND IT

J	F	M	A
M	J	**J**	A
S	O	N	D

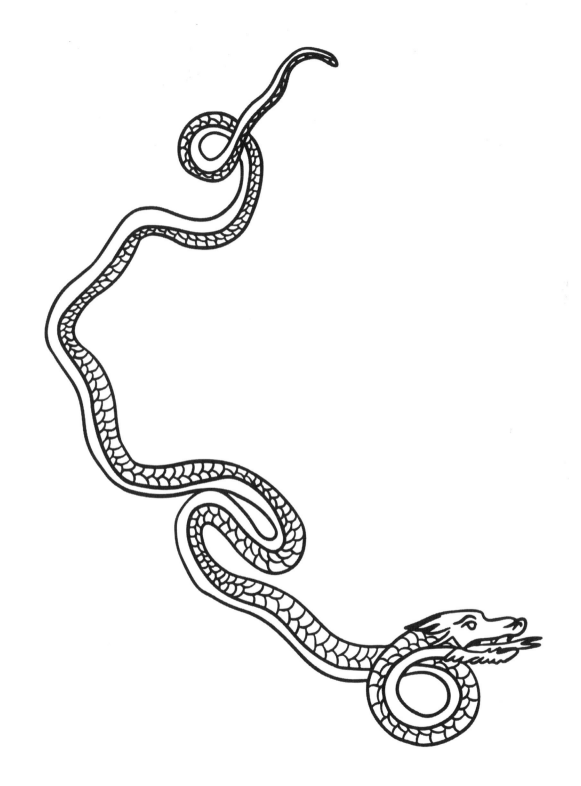

AURIGA

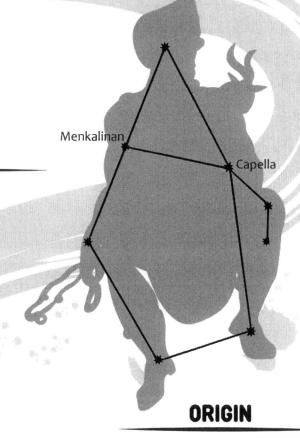

Menkalinan

Capella

SIZE IN THE NIGHT SKY

BIG

1274 times **X** the size of the full moon

DID YOU KNOW?

This constellation represents Erichthonius, son of Athena, who was regarded as the inventor of the four horse chariot.

BONUS FACT

Capella is the sixth brightest star in the night sky.

ORIGIN

ANCIENT GREECE

BEST TIME TO FIND IT

J	**F**	**M**	A
M	J	J	A
S	O	N	D

SEXTANS
(sextans)

SIZE IN THE NIGHT SKY

SMALL

609 times **X** the size of the full moon

DID YOU KNOW?

It was named after the sextant, which is an instrument astronomers used to measure the position of stars.

ORIGIN

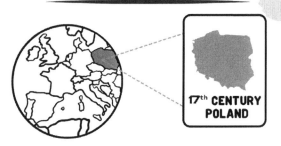

17th CENTURY POLAND

BEST TIME TO FIND IT

J	F	M	A
M	J	J	A
S	O	N	D

TAURUS
(bull)

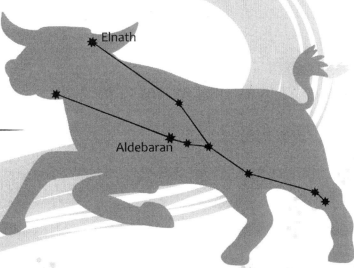

SIZE IN THE NIGHT SKY

BIG

1545 **X** the size of
times   the full moon

DID YOU KNOW?

Taurus is one of the oldest constellations, as it marks the location of the sun during the spring equinox. It was associated with a bull in Mesopotamia, Egypt, Greece and Rome.

ORIGIN

PREHISTORY

BEST TIME TO FIND IT

J	F	M	A
M	J	J	A
S	O	N	D

MONOCEROS

SIZE IN THE NIGHT SKY

SMALL

935 times **X** the size of the full moon

DID YOU KNOW?

Unlike other constellations named in the 16th century, the name is in Greek instead of Latin. Mono means single (think monocycle), ceros means horn (think Rhinoceros). In Latin its name would be Unicornis.

ORIGIN

16th CENTURY NETHERLANDS

BEST TIME TO FIND IT

J	**F**	M	A
M	J	J	A
S	O	N	D

AQUILA
(eagle)

The constellation Aquila with labeled stars: Altair, Tarazed, Okab

SIZE IN THE NIGHT SKY

BIG

1264 times X the size of the full moon

DID YOU KNOW?
The Greek Aquila is probably based on the Babylonian constellation of the Eagle.

BONUS FACT
people sometimes mistake this constellation for a seagull, which is a another constellation that is located nearby.

ORIGIN

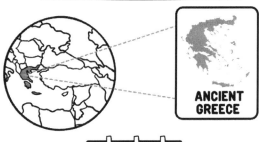

ANCIENT GREECE

BEST TIME TO FIND IT

J	F	M	A
M	J	J	**A**
S	O	N	D

CAPRICORNUS
(goat horn)

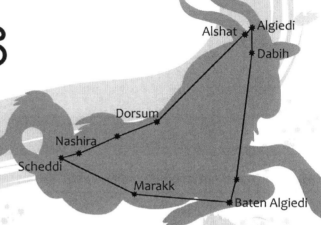

Alshat · Algiedi · Dabih · Dorsum · Nashira · Scheddi · Marakk · Baten Algiedi

SIZE IN THE NIGHT SKY

SMALL

803 times **X** the size of the full moon

DID YOU KNOW?

Capricornus represents Amalthea, a goat that fed milk to Zeus after being saved from Chronos. Amalthea's broken horn became the Cornucopia: a horn that provides infinite food.

BONUS FACT

In ancient times, the winter solstice occurred in this constellation. Due to the movement of the earth, the winter solstice now occurs in Sagittarius.

ORIGIN

GRECO-ROMAN

BABYLONIA
(modern Iraq and Syria)

BEST TIME TO FIND IT

J	F	M	A
M	J	J	A
S	O	N	D

CHAMAELEON

SIZE IN THE NIGHT SKY

TINY

256 X
times   the size of
         the full moon

ORIGIN

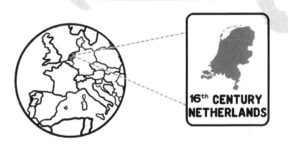

16ᵗʰ CENTURY
NETHERLANDS

DID YOU KNOW?

Chameleon represents a kind of lizard that can change color and extend its tongue twice the length of its body!

BEST TIME TO FIND IT

J	F	M	A
M	J	J	A
S	O	N	D

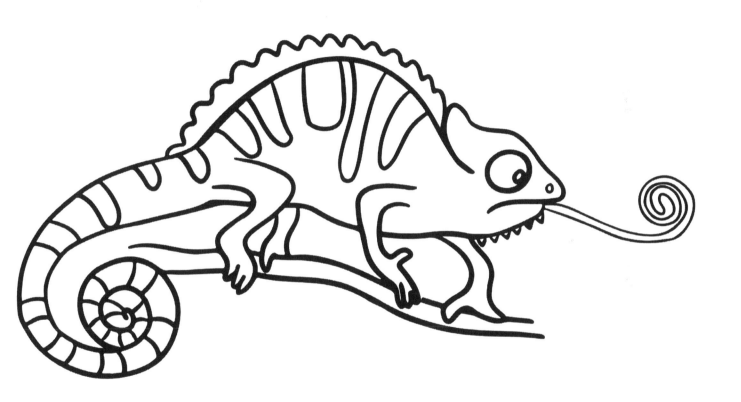

VOLANS
(flying)

SIZE IN THE NIGHT SKY
TINY

273 times **X** the size of the full moon

DID YOU KNOW?
The original name for this constellation was Piscis Volans, the flying fish. It was shortened to its current form in the 19th century.

ORIGIN

16th CENTURY NETHERLANDS

BEST TIME TO FIND IT

J	F	M	A
M	J	J	A
S	O	N	D

BOÖTES
(herder)

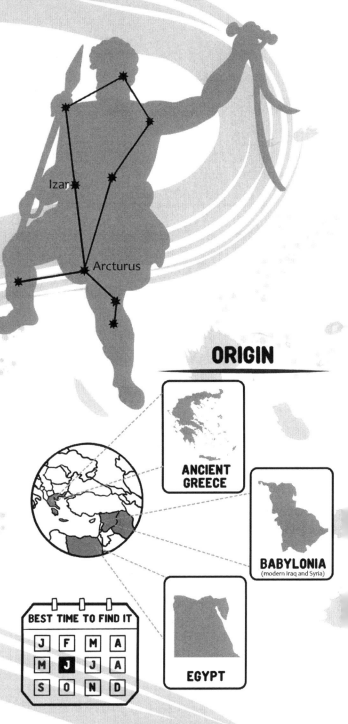

Izar
Arcturus

SIZE IN THE NIGHT SKY

BIG

1759 **X** the size of
times   the full moon

DID YOU KNOW?
Although the exact symbolism of the constellation is different across cultures, it has always been associated with farmers.

! **BONUS FACT**
Arcturus is the fourth brightest star in the sky, and is classified as giant star. It isn't as bright as the brightest three simply because its farther away.

ORIGIN

ANCIENT GREECE

BABYLONIA
(modern Iraq and Syria)

EGYPT

BEST TIME TO FIND IT

J	F	M	A
M	**J**	J	A
S	O	N	D

CANES VENATICI
(hunting dogs)

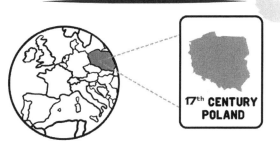

SIZE IN THE NIGHT SKY

SMALL

902 times **X** the size of the full moon

ORIGIN

17ᵗʰ CENTURY POLAND

DID YOU KNOW?

Due to a comical series of mistranslations, this constellation went from being a club held by Bootes (the herder), to a staff, to Bootes' dogs.

BONUS FACT

The name of this constellation was translated from Greek to Arabic and then to Latin.

BEST TIME TO FIND IT

J	F	M	A
M	J	J	A
S	O	N	D

LEO
(lion)

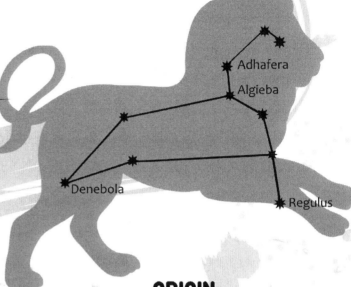

Adhafera
Algieba
Denebola
Regulus

SIZE IN THE NIGHT SKY

BIG

1836 times **X** the size of the full moon

DID YOU KNOW?

It represents the Nemean Lion, which was killed by Hercules as part of the twelve tasks.

BONUS FACT

The Persians, Turks, Syrians and Indians all considered this constellation to represent a lion.

ORIGIN

GRECO-ROMAN

BEST TIME TO FIND IT

J F M A
M J J A
S O N D

HYDRA

Ukdah

Alphard

Zhang

SIZE IN THE NIGHT SKY

HUGE

2527 **X** times   the size of the full moon

DID YOU KNOW?

The Greek myth tells of how Hercules defeated the Hydra as part of his twelve labors.

! **BONUS FACT**

In Babylonian mythology, the hydra was a creature formed by combining a lion, a snake and a bird.

ORIGIN

ANCIENT GREECE

BABYLONIA
(modern Iraq and Syria)

BEST TIME TO FIND IT

J	F	M	A
M	J	J	A
S	O	N	D

PHOENIX

Ankaa

SIZE IN THE NIGHT SKY

SMALL

909 times **X** the size of the full moon

DID YOU KNOW?

Unlike most constellations introduced by European astronomers in the 17th, 18th and 19th centuries, this constellation had a history in the ancient world, where people saw it as an ostrich, an eagle and even a boat.

ORIGIN

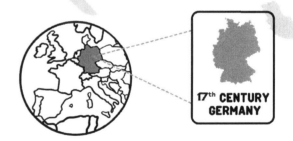

17TH CENTURY GERMANY

BEST TIME TO FIND IT

J	F	M	A
M	J	J	A
S	O	**N**	D

PISCES
(fishes)

Fum Al Samakah

Van Maanen's Star

Kullat Nunu

Alresha

SIZE IN THE NIGHT SKY

BIG

1724 times **X** the size of the full moon

DID YOU KNOW?

This constellation is associated with the legend of how Aphrodite (Venus) escaped with her son Eros (Cupid) from a monster by transforming themselves into a pair of fishes.

BONUS FACT

All constellations of the Zodiac are named in Latin despite being Greek in origin. The greek word for fishes is Ichthýes.

ORIGIN

GRECO-ROMAN

BEST TIME TO FIND IT

J	F	M	A
M	J	J	A
S	O	**N**	D

CANIS MINOR
(little dog)

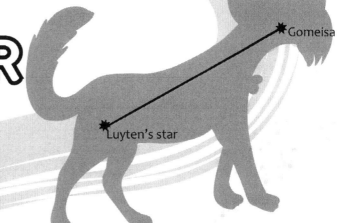

Gomeisa

Luyten's star

SIZE IN THE NIGHT SKY

TINY

355 times **X** the size of the full moon

DID YOU KNOW?

This constellations has been interpreted in many ways by the Greeks, Babylonians and Akkadians: a dog, a rooster, a pair of twin deities and even a fox.

ORIGIN

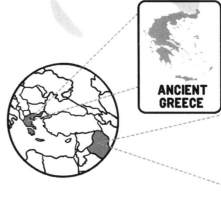

ANCIENT GREECE

MESOPOTAMIA
(Modern Iraq)

BEST TIME TO FIND IT

J	F	M	A
M	J	J	A
S	O	N	D

SCORPIUS
(scorpion)

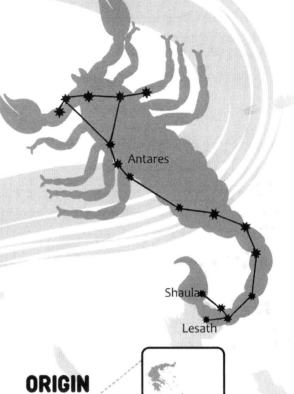

Antares

Shaula

Lesath

SIZE IN THE NIGHT SKY

SMALL

964 times **X** the size of the full moon

DID YOU KNOW?

In Greek Mythology, Scorpius was a giant scorpion sent by Artemis (the goddess of the hunt and wilderness) to fight Orion after he bragged about being the greatest hunter.

BONUS FACT

! For the Babylonians Scorpius was also a scorpion, although for them Libra represented Scorpius claws.

ORIGIN

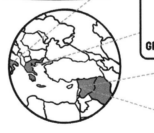

GRECO-ROMAN

BABYLONIA
(modern Iraq and Syria)

BEST TIME TO FIND IT

J	F	M	A
M	J	**J**	A
S	O	N	D

PAVO
(peacock)

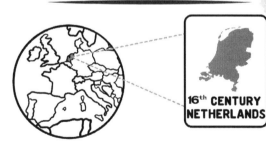

SIZE IN THE NIGHT SKY

SMALL

733 times **X** the size of the full moon

DID YOU KNOW?

For the ancient Greeks this constellation represented Argus, the shipbuilder, who was transformed into a peacock by the goddess Juno. We can only guess if it was coincidence or not.

ORIGIN

16ᵗʰ CENTURY NETHERLANDS

BEST TIME TO FIND IT

J	F	M	A
M	J	J	**A**
S	O	N	D

CORONA BOREALIS

SIZE IN THE NIGHT SKY

TINY

347 times **X** the size of the full moon

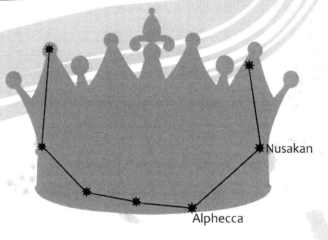

Nusakan

Alphecca

ORIGIN

DID YOU KNOW?

Corona Borealis represents a crown given by the god Dionysus to Princess Ariadne of Crete. Dionysus put the crown in the heavens to commemorate the weddding.

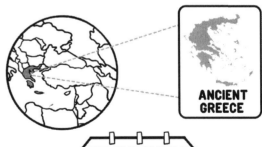

ANCIENT GREECE

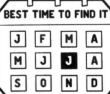

BEST TIME TO FIND IT

J	F	M	A
M	J	**J**	A
S	O	N	D

DELPHINUS
(dolphin)

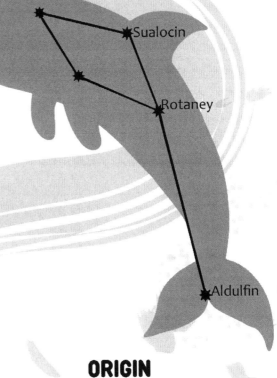

Sualocin

Rotaney

Aldulfin

SIZE IN THE NIGHT SKY
TINY

366 times **X** the size of the full moon

DID YOU KNOW?

Delphinus was a dolphin that helped the god Poseidon look for the woman he loved, after helping him find her he put the dolphin up in the heavens as a reward.

ORIGIN

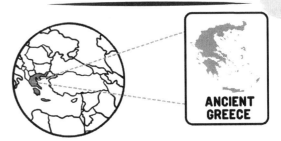

ANCIENT GREECE

BEST TIME TO FIND IT

J	F	M	A
M	J	J	A
S	O	N	D

URSA MINOR
(the little bear)

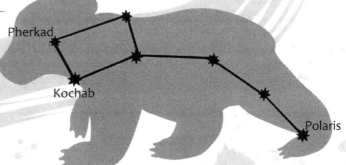

Pherkad

Kochab

Polaris

SIZE IN THE NIGHT SKY

TINY

496 times **X** the size of the full moon

ORIGIN

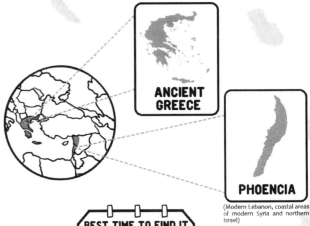

ANCIENT GREECE

PHOENCIA
(Modern Lebanon, coastal areas of modern Syria and northern Israel)

DID YOU KNOW?

Polaris, the brightest star in the constellation, always points to the north. Because of its use in navigation it's been important for many different cultures around the world.

BONUS FACT

Not everyone thought of a bear when looking at this constellation. For the Chinese it was a curved array, in English-speaking countries people refer to it as the Little Dipper.

BEST TIME TO FIND IT

J	F	M	A
M	**J**	J	A
S	O	N	D

CENTAURUS
(centaur)

Alpha Centauri

SIZE IN THE NIGHT SKY

HUGE

2055 **X**

times   the size of the full moon

ORIGIN

ANCIENT GREECE

DID YOU KNOW?

The constellation represents Chiron, a centaur who was the teacher of many mythological Greek heroes including Hercules, Theseus, and Jason -- the leader of the Argonauts.

BONUS FACT

Being only 4.27 light-years away, Alpha Centauri is the closest star system to earth!

BEST TIME TO FIND IT

J	F	M	A
M	J	J	A
S	O	N	D

DRACO
(dragon)

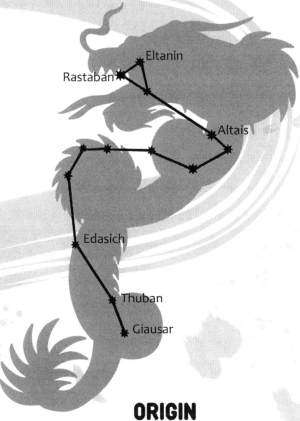

Eltanin
Rastaban
Altais
Edasich
Thuban
Giausar

SIZE IN THE NIGHT SKY

HUGE

2100 **X**
times   the size of
the full moon

DID YOU KNOW?

The constellation was inspired by Ladon, a dragon that Hercules defetaed in order to retrieve a golden apple that the dragon was guarding..

! **BONUS FACT**
In Greco-Roman legend, Draco was a dragon killed by the goddess Minerva.

ORIGIN

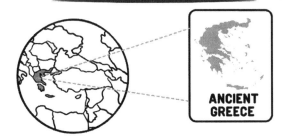

ANCIENT GREECE

BEST TIME TO FIND IT

J	F	M	A
M	J	**J**	A
S	O	N	D

GEMINI

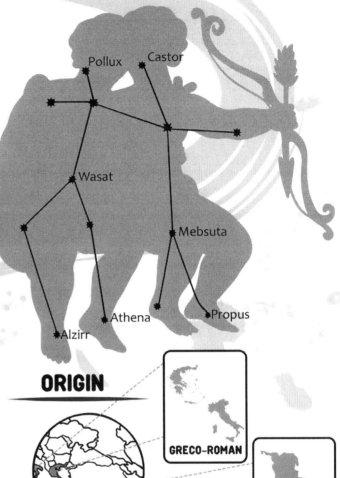

Pollux

Castor

Wasat

Mebsuta

Athena

Propus

Alzirr

SIZE IN THE NIGHT SKY

SMALL

997 times **X** the size of the full moon

DID YOU KNOW?

According to the ancient Greeks the two people in this constellation are the brothers Castor and Pollux.

In the Babylonian version they are two twin gods.

ORIGIN

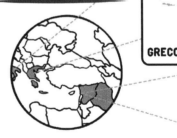

GRECO-ROMAN

BABYLONIA
(modern Iraq and Syria)

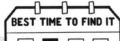

BEST TIME TO FIND IT

J	**F**	M	A
M	J	J	A
S	O	N	D

LYNX

Alsciaukat

SIZE IN THE NIGHT SKY

BIG

1057 **X**
times · the size of the full moon

DID YOU KNOW?

Johannes Hevelius named the constellation after this elusive animal because it's very difficult to see.

ORIGIN

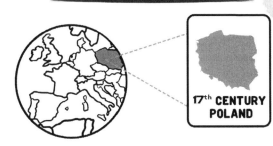

17ᵗʰ CENTURY POLAND

BEST TIME TO FIND IT

J	F	**M**	A
M	J	J	A
S	O	N	D

LEO MINOR
(little lion)

Praecipua

SIZE IN THE NIGHT SKY

TINY

450 times **X** the size of the full moon

ORIGIN

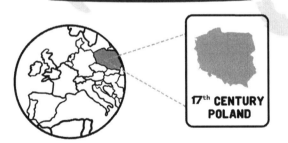

17ᵗʰ CENTURY POLAND

DID YOU KNOW?

The ancient Greeks described this region of the sky as having no constellations. Many centuries later Johannes Hevelius depicted it as a small lion that accompanies the big lion, Leo.

BEST TIME TO FIND IT

J	F	M	A
M	J	J	A
S	O	N	D

VIRGO

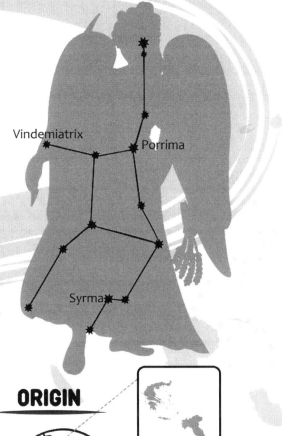

Vindemiatrix
Porrima
Syrma

SIZE IN THE NIGHT SKY

HUGE

2509 X
times   the size of
the full moon

DID YOU KNOW?

Virgo has been associated with a number of deities like the Babylonian Shala, The greek Demeter and the Roman Ceres.

!   **BONUS FACT**

Quasar 3C 273, the first quasar ever identified, is located inside this constellation.

ORIGIN

GRECO-ROMAN

BABYLONIA
(modern Iraq and Syria)

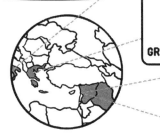

BEST TIME TO FIND IT

J	F	M	A
M	J	J	A
S	O	N	D

URSA MAJOR
(the big bear)

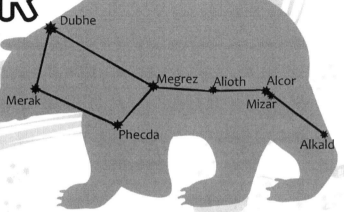

Dubhe
Merak
Phecda
Megrez
Alioth
Alcor
Mizar
Alkald

SIZE IN THE NIGHT SKY

HUGE

2482 **X**

times   the size of
the full moon

ORIGIN

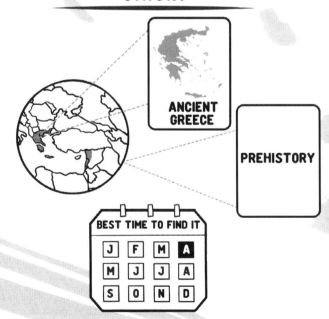

ANCIENT GREECE

PREHISTORY

DID YOU KNOW?

One of the biggest constellations in the sky. Much like Ursa Minor it's been an important constellation in many cultures. For the Greeks it was a bear, but it has received names such as The Wagon, The Plough and of course, The Big Dipper.

!

BONUS FACT

This constellation appears in the official flag of Alaska.

BEST TIME TO FIND IT

J	F	M	A
M	J	J	A
S	O	N	D

CANCER
(crab)

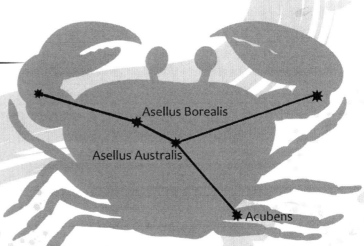

Asellus Borealis

Asellus Australis

Acubens

SIZE IN THE NIGHT SKY

SMALL

981 times **X** the size of the full moon

ORIGIN

ANCIENT GREECE

DID YOU KNOW?

Cancer is associated with a crab that bit Hercules in the foot while he was fighting the Hydra.

! BONUS FACT

Cancer is the Latin (Roman) word for crab, in Greek the name for crab is Karkinos

BEST TIME TO FIND IT

J	F	M	A
M	J	J	A
S	O	N	D

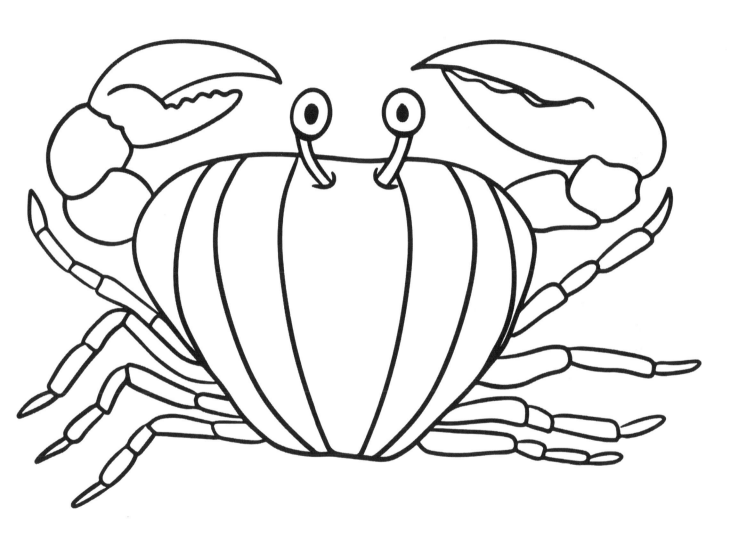

COLUMBA
(dove)

Phact

Wezn

SIZE IN THE NIGHT SKY

TINY

524 times **X** the size of the full moon

ORIGIN

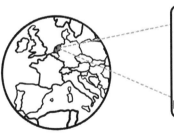

16th CENTURY NETHERLANDS

DID YOU KNOW?

This constellation was originally named Noah's Dove, referring to the bird that visited Noah in his ark at the end of the great flood.

BEST TIME TO FIND IT

J	**F**	M	A
M	J	J	A
S	O	N	D

CANIS MAJOR
(greater dog)

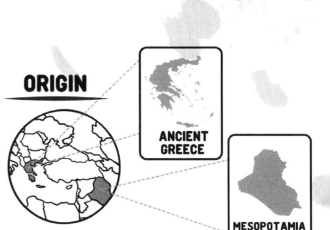

Adhara

Sirius

SIZE IN THE NIGHT SKY

SMALL

737 times **X** the size of the full moon

ORIGIN

ANCIENT GREECE

MESOPOTAMIA
(Modern Iraq)

DID YOU KNOW?

The most popular representation of Canis Major is that of Orion's dog. In some versions the dog is helping him fight Taurus the bull, in others it's chasing Lepus, the hare.

BONUS FACT

Sirius is the brightest star in the sky. It's very easy to spot!

BEST TIME TO FIND IT

J	F	M	A
M	J	J	A
S	O	N	D

ORION

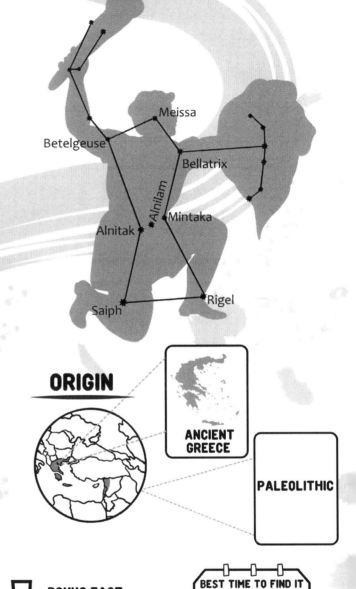

Betelgeuse
Meissa
Bellatrix
Alnitak
Alnilam
Mintaka
Saiph
Rigel

SIZE IN THE NIGHT SKY

BIG

1152 times **X** the size of the full moon

ORIGIN

ANCIENT GREECE

PALEOLITHIC

DID YOU KNOW?

Orion is one of the oldest constellations. There are carvings of Orion found in bones dating back 38,000 years!

In Greek mythology Orion is a great hunter, but many other cultures have given different interpretations to the constellation such as a shepherd for the Babylonians or a god for the Egyptians.

BONUS FACT
Orion is mentioned 3 times in the Bible.

BEST TIME TO FIND IT

J	F	M	A
M	J	J	A
S	O	N	D

ARIES
(ram)

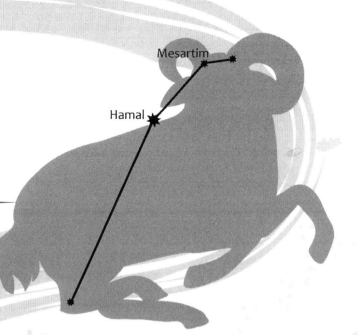

Mesartim

Hamal

SIZE IN THE NIGHT SKY

SMALL

855 times **X** the size of the full moon

DID YOU KNOW?

Although Aries has been associated with a ram since Babylonian times, for the Greeks it came to symbolize the golden ram, its fleece being an important part of the story of Jason and the Argonauts.

BONUS FACT

Aries is the Latin name for a ram, in Greek the name is émvolo

ORIGIN

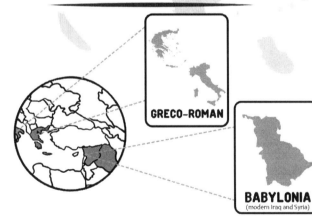

GRECO-ROMAN

BABYLONIA
(modern Iraq and Syria)

BEST TIME TO FIND IT

J	F	M	A
M	J	J	A
S	O	N	D

CAMELOPARDALIS

SIZE IN THE NIGHT SKY

BIG

1468 times **X** the size of the full moon

DID YOU KNOW?

Camelopardalis means giraffe in Latin, and comes from the combination of two Greek words: kamelo (camel) and pardalis (Spotted).

ORIGIN

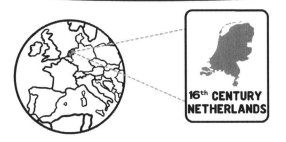

16th CENTURY NETHERLANDS

BEST TIME TO FIND IT

J	**F**	M	A
M	J	J	A
S	O	N	D

AQUARIUS
(water carrier)

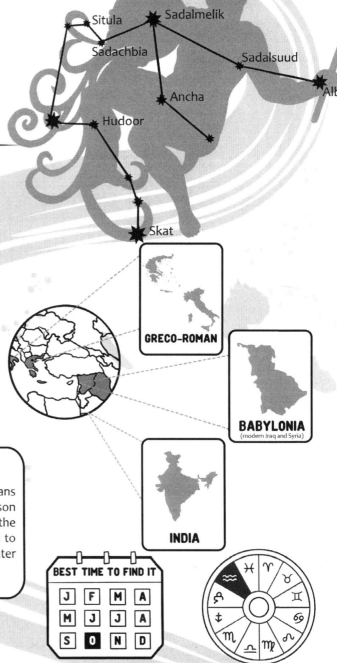

Situla
Sadalmelik
Sadachbia
Sadalsuud
Albali
Ancha
Hudoor
Skat

GRECO-ROMAN

BABYLONIA
(modern Iraq and Syria)

INDIA

SIZE IN THE NIGHT SKY
BIG

1900 times X the size of the full moon

DID YOU KNOW?

For the Babylonians and Indians Aquarius represented a person holding a pitch of water. For the Greeks the constellation came to represent a single vase with water pouring out of it.

BEST TIME TO FIND IT

J	F	M	A
M	J	J	A
S	O	N	D

VULPECULA
(little fox)

Anser

SIZE IN THE NIGHT SKY

TINY

520 times **X** the size of the full moon

ORIGIN

17ᵗʰ CENTURY POLAND

DID YOU KNOW?

This constellation originally consisted of a fox and a goose. Today the goose belongs to a separate constellation: Anser.

BONUS FACT

Although the goose belongs to a different constellation now, there's a star in Vulpecula whose name points to the old version.

BEST TIME TO FIND IT

J	F	M	A
M	J	J	A
S	O	N	D

VELA
(sails)

SIZE IN THE NIGHT SKY

SMALL

970 times **X** the size of the full moon

DID YOU KNOW?

Vela represents the sails on the ship Argo in which Jason and the Argonauts sailed when looking for the Golden Fleece.

ORIGIN

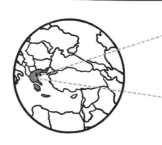 

ANCIENT GREECE

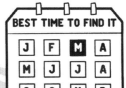

BEST TIME TO FIND IT

J	F	M	A
M	J	J	A
S	O	N	D

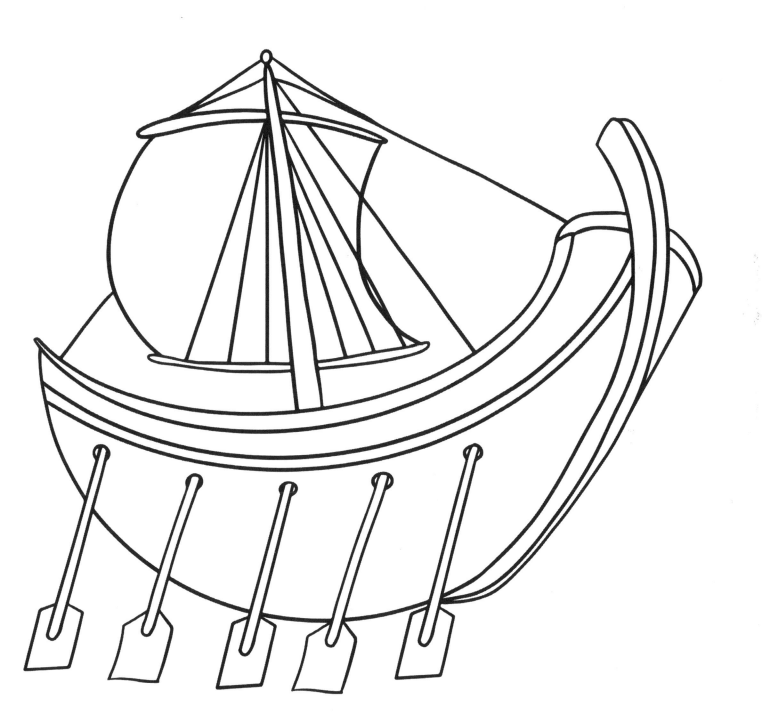

SAGITTARIUS
(archer)

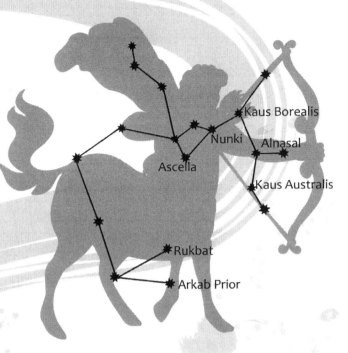

Kaus Borealis
Nunki
Alnasal
Ascella
Kaus Australis
Rukbat
Arkab Prior

SIZE IN THE NIGHT SKY

BIG

1681 times **X** the size of the full moon

DID YOU KNOW?

Sagittarius has always been represented as a centaur: half-man, half-horse. It isn't clear which archer it's supposed to represent.

BONUS FACT

Sagittarius is sometimes represented as a teapot. In good stargazing conditions, the Milky Way appears as steam coming out of it.

ORIGIN

GRECO-ROMAN

BABYLONIA
(modern Iraq and Syria)

BEST TIME TO FIND IT

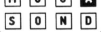

J	F	M	A
M	J	J	A
S	O	N	D

Mrs Mauve

Printed in Great Britain
by Amazon